He

REBECCA GOSS was born in
studied English at Liverpool John
in Creative Writing from Card
collection, *The Anatomy of Str*
Flambard Press. She has recently moved back to Suffolk after twenty
years in Liverpool, where she taught creative writing at Liverpool
John Moores University. She is married, has raised her two step-
children, and now combines writing full-time with caring for her
young daughter.

REBECCA GOSS

Her Birth

Northern House

CARCANET

First published in Great Britain in 2013 by
Northern House
In association with Carcanet Press Limited
Alliance House
Cross Street
Manchester M2 7AQ

www.carcanet.co.uk

A CIP catalogue record for this book is available from the British Library

ISBN 978 1 84777 238 1

The publisher acknowledges financial assistance from Arts Council England

Typeset by XL Publishing Services, Exmouth
Printed and bound in England by SRP Ltd, Exeter

This book is dedicated to my family: Jim, Jamie, Rosie, Molly, Diana, Richard, Katherine, William, George, Rosa, AJ, Lucy, Sebastian, Oliver, Joan and Jack.

I would like to share the dedication with:

Dr Ian Peart, Gill McBurney, Dr Emma Twigg, all staff on Ward K2 and O1 Clinic and the Intensive Care Unit at Alder Hey Children's NHS Foundation Trust, Dr Yoxall and staff on the Neonatal Unit at Liverpool Women's NHS Foundation Trust, Ruth Williams, Linda Brosnan, Kip Crooks, Penny Maginn, Grace, Rebecca, Rubén, Albert and last but by no means least, the Chattertons.

I would like to mention the people who loved Ella and are missed themselves: Clare Bennett, John Goss, Joan Rees and Leslie Driscoll.

I would like to thank the following for their help and encouragement: Jim, Jon Glover, John Whale, Will Mackie, Andrew Forster, Kate Clanchy, Penny Feeny, Gail and David Aubrey, Ann Chalmers and Sarah Maclennan.

I am very grateful for the financial support of The Society of Authors, and to Pan Macmillan for permission to reproduce the extract from Kate Clanchy's poem 'Infant'.

And Ella, 21st March 2007–5th August 2008. High-five sweetheart.

Contents

Echo

Fetal Heart   13
Room in a Hospital   14
Skin-to-Skin   15
Toast   16
Clinic   17
Echo   18
Palliative   19
A Dream of Heart Babies   20
I Sweat When I   21
Swings   22
Ward at Night   23
Severe Ebstein's Anomaly   24
A Child Dies in Liverpool   25
Post   26
St Mary's   27
Her Birth   28

Mining

The Postmistress   31
Honey   32
Stretch Marks   33
The Highchair   34
Print   35
Mining   36
You're Lucky You Can Dream About Her   37
October   38
Muscovado Sugar   39
My Neighbour's Himalayan Birch   40
The 21st of March   41
Mothers of the Dead   42
Found   43
Helpline   44
The Lights   45

Sunday Papers   46
Grief Goes Jogging   47
Peeing at the Odeon   48
Repair   49
Another   50

Welcome

Why We Had Another Baby   53
Test   54
Hyperemesis Gravidarum   55
As Owls Do   56
Clothes   57
Welcome   58
Shadows   59
My Animal   60
Lost   61
Bench   62
Telling the Tale   63
In Memory of John Ernest Goss 1920–2011   64
Snail   65
Moon   66
Taking You There   67
Last Poem   68

Acknowledgements   70

Soon, you will make your way out
of this estuary country, leave
the low farms and fog banks, tack through
the brackish channels and long
reed-clogged rivulets, reach
the last turn, the salt air and river mouth,
the wide grey sea beyond it.

Kate Clanchy, 'Infant', from *Newborn*

Echo

Fetal Heart

It uncurled, unfolded
into four but was clover
with an unlucky lobe,
the rarest of anomalies
that would flourish
to defeat her.

Room in a Hospital

No tabloids, no vending cups, no debris
of the bored and hungry. Instead
carpet, fireplace, neat homely items.

This is not the room where you wait for news,
this is the room where you are told it.

At the coffee table, the doctor hunches
to draw a heart. It needs time from his pen,
crossings out and a white space

where the valve won't meet.
The heart is thirty-six hours old and hers.

Perched on cool leather, we puzzle the sketch,
my husband takes his glasses off to cry.
Our daughter warrants a new vocabulary

and we are struggling to learn.

Skin-to-Skin

Wrapped inside my gown
her hot pearl of cheek

sticks against my chest,
her knees dent the dough

of my stomach until a registrar
comes to incubate, must find

a vein beneath luminous skin,
his arms gowned, his hands gloved.

Toast

Hunger sends us seeking its cheap white thickness,
forces us to leave her, two days old, incubated

in Neonatal and stand in the 'parents' kitchen'.
Fluorescent lit, poky, we embrace the closest thing

to home, busy ourselves separating slices, re-washing
plates. I take two squares of butter from the fridge,

warm their foil corners in my fists. Fear rolls in my shrunken
gut, watching you, wanting our sad mouths to kiss.

You spread, cut and pass me a golden triangle,
the oily joy of it leaking onto fingers. We suck it down

into machinery that made her, wondering where the fault is.

Clinic

We wait to be called
and watch a toddler,
bare for a nappy,
playing at the toy table,
a raw, linear scar
in the centre
of his chest.

I picture him
dulled to a floppy
sleep, slit like a fish
for a surgeon
to cup his heart,
take its damaged
weight and begin.

Echo

Not the one that starts in your mouth, bounces back,
rolls down your throat, vowels collecting like balls in a net.

I mean an echocardiogram. The doctor's probe plays
slim keys of her ribs, draws the murmur of music

that beats in there. Her baby heart dances on the screen.
If only it was lucky to see this secret cave. A deformed

valve leaps between chambers like a March hare,
marking the spring day she was born. Diverted on its travels,

her blood is a mystery trail, leaving me lost.
I distract her with bubbles. Keep clear spheres

coming around her head, wanting them to last,
each pop a small, inexplicable loss.

Palliative

I knew what it meant, but that didn't stop me:
I came home from clinic, early in her life,

sat on the stairs with my hardback *Collins*
solid as a baby on my knee, thumbed quickly

through papery leaves, whispering *l, m, n, o, p,*
to seek the word they said once

when discussing the flawed mechanics
of her heart. There, on a gauzy page,

its definition printed across shadows
of my fingers, I read *'serving to palliate'*,

(from Latin *pallium*, a cloak) and turned back
to find 'palliate' *vb* 1. *to lessen the severity*

of (pain, disease etc.) without curing
and I re-read *without curing* until *curing*

didn't look like *curing* anymore,
it looked like *curling* and I clasped my hands

around my knees, pulled that book hard
against my gut. As a student I loved its reams

of indisputable fact, its ability to reveal
and make clear. Now I bury its bulk

on the shelves, swathe myself in hope.

A Dream of Heart Babies

(a poem for their mothers)

Gathered on deck,
we slip them from our hands

like they slipped from our legs,
a shoal of heart babies

sweep down the hull.
Their fragile beats

thrum the keel, beats we've
often pressed our ears to,

seen tremble in dozing chests.
Here, they plunge and soar

in gregarious mass,
skins of cyanotic sheen.

Their pulses echo
for nautical miles,

in a search for chambers
more complex than coral.

We cut through ocean,
nets trailing the stern,

see our babies somersault
the spot we must haul.

The catch rises, drips
and bulges, spills glistening

infants, like oysters at our feet.
Each one cups a new heart

and we wonder every accurate throb.

I Sweat When I

Hoover. Mash potatoes. Fuck.
She sweats sitting up. Eight kilograms

and able to spread a stain on her
father's shirt, asleep in his arms.

A breastfeed left us slippery, hot,
her heart working harder

than mine. Weaning her
was undocumented. No chapters

for a child who can't eat.
I prepare another bottle,

blonde floss of her hair
sticky at her neck,

while she watches, breathes.

Swings

Swinging her

        in the park,

her fingers

        wrapped tight

on the bar,

        her smile bigger

than my heart;

        it must have been

such a thrill

        to swoop

and fall like that,

        for a child

who couldn't

        crawl, walk,

even pull up

        against my shin,

how free

        she must have been

then, on the swing.

Ward at Night

Composed in her lungs, the cough
scales her throat, stops her from sleeping.

I scoop her from her metal cot and rest
her broken heart on mine. Televisions hang

like planets overhead, as we creep past beds,
hear the cadenced breath of babies

through the bars. Bright at the ward's core,
the nurses' station beams help from its hub –

women who mark my baby's decreasing
growth, report to a cluster of registrars.

Eventually, she dozes. A nurse tacks a plaster
to her toe, restarts the monitor, to follow

this small satellite, failing in my arms.

Severe Ebstein's Anomaly

The lack of a cure sparked dreams.
In one, her father and I set out

for the island of disease beating
in her body. Her breath in our sails,

we navigated waves of excess fluid,
toured the ruins of her lungs.

Gradually propelled to the heave
of her heart's edge, I laid my hand

on its plump shore. Her father
kissed my brow, kitbag swung

across his back, and trekked towards
the faulty, flapping dam

of her tricuspid valve. There,
he gazed into the chamber

with its swish of redirected river
and set about his sole desire

to fix her. In intensive care,
as she fails in her father's arms,

doctors run to swarm her, apply
repeated pressure to her chest.

We flounder in the doorway,
lose sight of her small body

until a man, head bent, his mouth
aflood with tender vowels,

tugs us to her bedside to grant him
the undocking and let her come adrift.

A Child Dies in Liverpool

We are tourists now, in her home city,
but there was no last-minute booking
or excited packing of a case.
With pockets void of tour guides, we drift
to the waterfront we know well;
each dome and bronzed wing tip
blurred in gauzy grief. Stilled by rain,
we find a bench, sit down where her death
has docked us. Going home, back down
the river road, will be a foreign route without her.

Post

Who knew to trap the Inland Revenue's
slim brown demands inside a sorting office

for a few more days? Who let them lie
in the dark with promises from Barclays,

requests from BT? Who made sure
it was just the cards that came?

Twenty at a time, hitting vestibule tiles
with a heavy slap. I scooped them

from that cool place to our bed, where
her breath used to be. Those breaths

you counted (her five to your one),
as she slept between us, propped up

to keep the fluid down. Cards pile in clouds
of duvet. *Little one, sent among us briefly,*

your spirit meant to fly. Her cough
still rises from the sheets, from pools

in her lungs; her struggling wings.

St Mary's

Keeping the hem
of my new black dress
held up, I perch to pee
while a verger waits
patiently outside.
Close to my knee
a brick wall is
painted palest pink
and music I chose,
in that surreal
week, planning this
service for my child,
is coming through the clay.
People are entering
the church. Her funeral
has started. I cannot stop it.

Her Birth

On the wall, petunias,
painted in Walberswick.
I call to you, say
That's a good omen,
that's a good sign,
before buckling,
gripping the hospital bed.

Walberswick is where
I holidayed, every childhood
summer. It's where we announced
the news. Sixteen months
after the effort of her birth,
we collect a faux-walnut
box from Jenkins & Sons.
Inside, a clear sachet,
weightless as dried herbs.

We drive two hundred
and eighty-one miles
for that cold, unstoppable
wave to suck the sachet clean
and I ask you, *She is all right now,*
isn't she? She is all right?

Mining

The Postmistress

She said the river lured him to lie.
The day he slipped from her, stayed out

as the rain fell and fell, the village
bracing itself for change. There was

a boat, then it was gone. As the story
went on, my husband and I, tourists

in this empty post office, could only listen.
I saw her run to that swelling, every breath

sucking in hair. As she reached stepping stones,
saw the boat, his friends and finally him, alive,

I pretend to share relief in my envious mouth.
I want fear to breed like that in my sweat,

want my daughter, two weeks dead,
back here to grow, run, alarm me.

Honey

Gleaned from her own hives, a woman
who'd never met my daughter
but heard she'd gone, left a jar resting
on my step in August sun. A script
of instructions slipped beneath hot glass:
it was to be opened occasionally, inside
the scent of one last spring, preserved.
I roll its gold against light, picture the woman
bent at my door, but have never dared
to twist the lid, afraid the perfume of bees
might hurl me back to the garden; my daughter's
warm exhaustion in my arms. What if the lid's small pop
meant the vapour was lost? It would be my fault –
unable to keep an entire season in my lungs.

Stretch Marks

My swims kept those scars at bay,
two thousand lengths it took, to form

my mapless globe. No trace she was here,
her travels around me refused to surface

as she dived between poles, lapped
that black belly ocean. Once born, meridian

of my achievements, she went off course.
I followed her divergent route, but this was not

her geography. I have wished for them,
a record of her tracks, all snowed over, gone.

The Highchair

Fastened in its straps,
she craved my breast

like a new lamb.
Denied the breath

to chew or swallow,
her limbs did not puff

with weight, her neck taut
from the chin as she failed

to bloom. I'd announce
'Lunchtime!', in my

hopeful tone; she sat
grumpy as a gnome,

shook her head. The highchair
went to Sure Start.

Homemade stews
hurled frozen in a bin bag,

until it was lumpy with waste.

Print

We have her prints.

Hands and feet, pencil grey,
as if they stood her in soot.

A nurse lifted her palms
then soles to the paper.

Underneath, wrote her name,
the date. I wanted her handprint

to come home on sugar paper:
bright yellow, ready for the fridge.

Months later, the sun picked out
her paw on the pane, each tip,

tiny as peas. I peered close,
nose almost touching my fossil,

backlit on the glass.

Mining

I let socks dot the washing, coats grace
a chair's arm. Her hospital bag, too hard
to unpack, stayed slumped and ignored

but eventually there was a gathering,
the limp outline of her size carried upstairs.
It accumulated in the cot, a cold pit

of pyjamas, dresses, jeans. My heap of her,
visible through bars. Insides of sleeves
brushed with her cells, last flecks compacting

in pastel matter, until her father found me
fretting at its edge, suggested it was time
for the careful mining of her things.

Our intention to sort, fold and label soon became
a quick, unhappy shoving into grey plastic bags,
the silent hoisting to an attic's dark. Her cot

collapsed, I sobbed in that desolated space,
while my desk was carried in, books and pens
planted on its surface, her father's wise reclamation

of the site. I kept a row of lilac-buttoned relics
in my wardrobe. Hand-knitted proof, something
to haul my sorry lump of heart and make it blaze.

You're Lucky You Can Dream About Her

and I haven't got the nerve
to tell this woman, twenty years
bereft, that I don't like it. Unlike her
who longs to see the early shape
she held for only hours, I reject
the narratives that come at night.
In one, my baby's back to life
and hungry, but my cupboards
store thick dust on their shelves.
Days are hard enough, fifteen hours
strewn with her image. In my bed
I want peace. A little time before
the first blink brings up her hospital
death, the dark hollow of her pram.

October

Fingers hooked in milk bottles,
rinsed ready for their crate,

I open my front door
and I'm struck by the earthy

stink of autumn. That first promise
of cold; it comes like a scarf

tightening and I slam the door,
aborting this doorstep launch

into my best-loved month, without her.

Muscovado Sugar

I reach for the new kilogram bag, slick
with plastic wrap, clutch its bulk in both hands.
She weighed the same as eight of these,
at the time of her death. The mass her father
carried to intensive care, flanked by medics gifting
oxygen to her lips, and I walked behind, able to see
her crown, her father's competent back, conscious

of my arm, of someone's grip. I should scissor
this bag open, ease crystal heaps onto scales,
but I'm stuck in an imaginary stacking. Eight bags
cradled elbow to elbow, her cardinal number
stretching across my breast, carried up the stairs,
to lie down on the bed, pull the covers over us.
Imagine a yielding, imagine her move.

My Neighbour's Himalayan Birch

I watched him plant it, water it, bed it down
with his boot. It was another four years

before she was conceived, born, diagnosed
and brought home. I like to think the catkins

quivered in celebration when I carried her inside,
fragile as moth. Branches veined the sky

twenty metres from her cot and I envied
his reward; what my neighbour's patience brought him

as he nurtured with mulch, watched
its silver trunk stand up from the ground.

It swayed over all our comings and goings:
the year of dog walks (river-bound),

our grateful steer through seasons
then the increased trips to clinic,

its tremble above the funeral car.
This autumn, I notice its skeleton of bark

and think of other deciduous things:
antlers, wings, her teeth that never came.

The 21st of March

What
to do on
birthdays?
The whole day
to navigate, replaying
the birth but with no child's
hair to plait, no party, no cake.
We bought a yellow paper lantern
and waited for the dark. I was so anxious
it might tear but it was you who carried her to sea,
you who took off your shoes, waded in with that pocket
of ash. I trusted you then as I do now, to tug this concertina'd
frame, make a flame, allow it to swell below your fingers.
Plump with light, it sways with new and eager strength.
You let it go, to float above the garden chairs, the shed,
the tidy lawns of sleeping neighbours. It makes
a turn towards the Mersey and we're on tiptoes,
at the end of this eightieth day, watching our
own small sun head towards the river.
A very private equinox as it crosses
that fluvial division to surf new
latitudes and expire
from our
sight.

Mothers of the Dead

We're not necessarily destined
to attach like sorry limpets,
clinging to our similar facts.

I spoke to one on the phone,
her toddler fine one minute,
gone the next.

We knew each other's stories
but the call was about
a house-sale:

she wanted to buy mine.
I pushed my ear against
the phone, yearned

coded loss in her voice,
a shivering inflection
only I would understand

but it was an unremarkable
exchange. We breathed
in and out like normal women

before hanging up,
getting on with our lives.

Found

It surfaced like a dead fish
on my desk – top of the sachet
we sliced open to let her ashes spill.

It came into view
beneath a year of papers,
her name typed and stapled

to the edge. Stunned to see
I had some of her left
I studied the bits of grit

inside the rim – her toys, a book,
letters tucked in with her.
It happened quickly – my index finger

swabbed inside the plastic
until its tip was dark.
The other hand pulled open my shirt,

found the damp cave under my arm.
With one wipe, I smeared her
into pores, left my desk to go downstairs

knowing she had somehow been ingested.

Helpline

I've been told of women in their eighties
who dial on birthdays, their story drawn

from the receiver in small damp breaths:
'He would have been sixty'

and a voice wraps them in a blanket of vowels.
Somehow, a child has slipped from them.

They were unable to stop it, like sand collapsing
back down the hole, dug on that dry part of beach.

The Lights

Pausing in traffic, I'm miles away
when a file of children forces me
to focus. School now behind them,
they cross in a bustle of coats and bags –
their ages vague to me, but their limbs
bold and flailing, affirming themselves
with shoves and pushes. I marvel
this mass of certainty. Even the loners

get to the other side, lights turning green
as they dawdle. I'm beginning to realise
most children make it. It's rare to see
your child being fought for in intensive care;
to stay with her afterwards, saying her name.
It's unusual, at the undertakers, to finalise
arrangements then fumble for a photograph,
so they could know her when she was warm.

Sunday Papers

The feature I keep flicking past
finally lures me in – three mothers,
each with a dead teenage son.

One mother wears his clothes
around the house. Astonished
at her pluck, I'm flung back

to those early months,
scared to catch a dangling cuff
and reawaken threads.

Then a friend's weepy visit
in my sunlit porch, her sudden grab
for the small pink coat.

Freed from its stationary droop,
she rammed her hand inside the sleeve
and held it to her face. The gesture

left me open-mouthed as she nosed
my dead child's scent – so uncurbed,
so unabashed about her loss.

Grief Goes Jogging

You rise alongside me, as I tighten
my dressing gown belt.
Don't think about climbing inside
to cling on for the day,
trapping me in a fug of sad fibres.

I scrabble in drawers, find you
some shorts, a jogger's top,
zip the polyester tight at your throat.
You fight me with furious ankles,
but I force on trainers, make you

bounce on the spot. At the door,
I send you with a shove, shouting
'Bear left! Head for the river!'
See the promenade you've made
me walk plenty enough,

sometimes at dawn, in tears.
You pound my empty street,
sly back already bent. Hours later,
I find you wretched on the step.
You stink of pity and sweat.
I know you will come back in,

slip your arms around me,
but for now I leave you there.
See how you like it,
your head throbbing with hurt.
Discover the effort required
to haul yourself straight.

Peeing at the Odeon

I exit the cubicle and catch myself in fluorescent light.
Glare exposes grief's attack: a web of lines around
the eyes, evidence of arrested sleep, ageing each
unhappy ball. Beside me, teenagers jostle for taps,
hungry for their own reflections. Why should they
know desire for a child, how complicated it might be?
These girls' futures stretch no further than the boys
who line the foyer. I dampen hands with my head down,
my husband waiting with tickets for Screen Two.
Relieved to see him, I grip his arm and hurry for the dark.

Repair

for Jim

The day we married, you kissed me on our lawn,
toasted by a crowd; both of us heady with expectation.

We have since buried our child and edged
to that inevitable brink, the end of our marriage

a possibility, a rumour considered by those same
wedding guests: *what a shame, what bad luck*

but you went for therapy, some time alone,
a night class. There, you studied other makers

then jabbed at a plane, its thick, ejected coils
looping at your wrist. Soon, a paper-thin shaving

could quiver in your palm, evidence of a new skill.
We considered that gap in the garden, paced its perimeter,

mugs of tea cooling in our hands. The workshop nestles
in its corner, honeysuckle licks the roof and from a window

I watch you walk inside, know you are bent at the bench,
able and making, sawdust coating you like down.

Another

Assure me I will be ripe
and stretching, my belly full

but still have space
for her first days, last days.

Assure me I will keep her toes
accurate as maths, her smell

precise, her voice heard above birds.
Assure me I will not howl her name

during birth, that I will place
newborn fingers in my mouth,

taste only newness.
Then, I will consider another.

Welcome

Why We Had Another Baby

The fear that one day
we might stand with

a bed or table between us,
some domestic setting

where I'm wrapped in a towel
or lifting a lasagne from the oven

and you accuse me of never
getting over it and I accuse you

of never getting over it
and that this might take place

in a house of empty bedrooms
or very small flat (because we

won't need the space and even the dog
might be dead),

the fear that neighbours get used
to our puffy unhappiness.

It is the fear of that
that leads us to our bed,

where you kiss my empty hands
and very slowly I anticipate.

Test

Pink with piss, a damp wand
rests above the sink, as instructed.

I sit my thighs on a cold bath's edge
and in those two minutes

scan the row of dusty children's books
as they tilt beside the mirror.

Fifteen months since they scattered
the floor, her pyjamas warming

on the radiator. Her naked squirm
in steamy fug as the water ran,

my quick glances at her chest,
how the ribs worked as she breathed.

Then she disappeared. A foretold vanishing,
yet it floored us still. I'm not sure how

we stoppered sadness to make another.
I stand to blow the book-spines clean

then turn towards the sink. Two blue lines
and there you are, emerging, like magic.

Hyperemesis Gravidarum

You made me sick. Sicker than the ferry
to France, the back seat to Skye,
the Christmas Eve drinks of 2003.
My kitchen housed a fog of toxic cloud,
making me vomit on dishes slung
in the sink. I'd lurch towards hedges
when walking the dog, retch into bags
at red traffic lights, until a friend drove me,
cracked-lipped and ashen, to Emergency
where they found me a bed, a drip,
an ultrasound slot. I watched you
on the screen: unreal as a pixie, guiltless
as good news, a flourish in my body of bile.

As Owls Do

Wrapped in yourself like a spool,
Trawling your dark, as owls do.
— Sylvia Plath

The probe sweeps through gel on my stomach
as we come into your cave, try to prompt you
into flight. Everyone is silent, as you gradually
uncurl and, with a noiseless twist of your head,
turn your black eyes on us. I feel hunted, caught;
fear you can sense the ambivalence in me.

Four months from now, I'm hoping I will love you
each time I find you, usurping another's cot.
The midwife holds a file, the sad biography
of my procreative life. My ability to bear
the unhealthy means the doctor must locate
a lump of thumping muscle, see through dark

to all its tiny workings. We're told this featherweight
of baby will survive. My husband grips my hand
and we comprehend the wingbeats of your heart.

Clothes

Left in a loft, a baby's clothes will yellow.
That's what I was told and I thought of my

dead baby's things, stuffed into sacks,
stirring with a benign mould. A year later

and pregnant, I yanked plastic bags
from their muggy, attic dark. Spilled

them like Christmas sacks and picked
my way through sleep suits, patchy

with promised lemon stains. Vests
scabbed with breakfast, crusted proof

of meals and my shock at dirty things.
But why would I have come home,

numb from intensive care, and set about
washing what she left behind?

I selected neutral colours, an array of small
things for the unknown sex of my bud,

only to creep back later and delve for the pink,
a last hopeful load. Spun dry and flapping

on a line, my longing exposed in a string
of rosy pennants, ready to hail her, wrap her tight.

Welcome

to Molly, 2010

For those secret hours, she was just ours.
No-one else knew about my breaths
(deep, hard, long) to spill her, soft as mole

into the light. Her crawl across my chest to drink
untold, we let the world stay furled in sleep
to hold her. As dawn swelled behind curtains

we thought of a name. It came in chorus,
as if we had always known and carried it
under tongues for nine months, only now

its round vowel released into the room.
With your lips at her ear, you let syllables
slide into flooded canals, named her

over and over while outside, Mersey gulls
swooped in semi-dark, cawing their applause.

Shadows

Clasping your newborn ribs
I see *her* small bones
beneath your skin.

Your dead sister, visible
like x-ray, is glowing
through your pores.

There were so many x-rays.
Machine brought in
to the ward, its clunky

bulk swamped her cot
like a monster. Nurses
cloaked me in lead

and I held up her tiny wrists,
exposed her gasping
to the gamma.

You breathe differently.
You *are* different
but during night feeds,

your vertebrae's curve
against my arm,
you are the same baby,

warm with marrow,
sucking for your life.

My Animal

Amphibian, how you swam
to get here. Left the pond
of your gestation in a rush

of slime. Not quite the blind worm
you were, squirming in light; now
the greedy chick mouthing

for my breast. I clasp you there,
feel your piglet's suck. The skin
on your back velvet as mole

as your nails claw for more.
I turn you upright, pat you
till you purr. It's visceral, this love.

Lost

Walking with my baby in the park and slowing for someone
I hadn't seen in years, I heard myself interrupting coos
to say, *You know I lost my first child, don't you?*

As if there were a possibility she might turn up again,
with my glove or best pen. That a sweep of the sofa
might reward me her hand, then body, pulled from the gap

between cushions. As if all I did was lose sight of her.
That an anxious scan of sand could bring her into focus,
squat and peering at shells. As if I could swear

I had hold of her earlier, that a frantic spill of my bag
would bear lip gloss, chewing gum, keys and I'd be
unable to explain, apologising for my dreadful mistake.

As if one day, I could run from my house, screaming 'Found!'
Lift her for the whole road to see, shouting 'Here she is! Here she is!
                                                    She is here!'

Bench

I'm past them in seconds, but what I see
leaks inside my brain to spoil the afternoon:

three women, settled in the sun, legs swung
beneath wooden slats, rocking a pram each.

I envy everything about them: their easy chatter
as they lull small bodies, the sphere of belly

on the dark-haired one, a second child coming
to run with her first. I get angry that I'm walking

with one child instead of two. I want to ruin
their tranquil hour, tell them my dead daughter

should be five by now. I consider the stillbirths
and miscarriages that could exist between them

(as if tragedy might make me kinder)
but no, I'm the only one to have suffered.

Downwind, three women lean forward to watch
a mother push her pram in furious strides,

slipstream of long hair tangling and in the air
they smell self-pity, its clear and definite stench.

Telling the Tale

One day, I will beckon with a finger,
curl you on my lap, tell the story
of your sister's sleep, unbroken
by a kiss. I'll describe the dawn
we cheered at her arrival; bowed
to beauty, grace and song until a scan
revealed the wicked gift of Ebstein's
and we watched for sixteen anxious
months, brambles thickening at her heart,
with no way through to save her.

In Memory of John Ernest Goss 1920–2011

*I want to be cremated and my ashes thrown in the air. Straight from
the flames to the winds, and let that be that.*

— the closing lines of *Akenfield*, by Ronald Blythe

As you wobble the length of our hall, hand fiercely tight
in mine, your great-grandfather is letting go.

His seven stones of bone barely dent the bed. His lips kept wet
by a nurse's sponge, his hand held warm by his son.

I consider the efforts of your respective breaths –
his faint, yours eager – as you pad small steps,

adopt a penguin's gait. Between you, a gap of ninety years,
storing its wars and discoveries, far reaching

as the moon he lived beneath. In the *little arable kingdom*
he chose for home, he married, raised a boy in sunken lanes;

stayed rooted in its loamy soils, grew as ancient as its woods.
You pick up pace and race towards the mirror. If there was time,

this news of your early steps would be recorded, folded,
delivered overnight. Hand-written word from his kin, he loved

the language of lives elsewhere. He has a wish to star the air
on a stretch of Suffolk coast and we will take him, in the throng

of family he has sprung. For now, I watch you in the glass,
behind us see the hall, the pram, how far we've come.

'little arable kingdom' – Blythe's description of East Anglia

Snail

Bending as toddlers do (palms on knees,
bottom skimming the ground) you gaze
at the snail. Our well-trodden route
around the block is subject to pauses
like these. Your scour for pavement
treasure can delay a letter's posting
as you pick up petals, ponder twigs.

Historically, I've plucked a snail's suck
from precious stems, tossed it into soil.
Now, I'm as curious as you are, absorbed
in its squirm, its feelers growing just for us.
With my hand on your back, I point to the shell,
its house of heart, liver, kidney, lung.
We are mesmerised, in no rush to get home.

Moon

All day you've waited,
running from one end

of the house to the other,
as if controlled by its distant

pull. After bath, blanket
at your shoulders, we duck

the washing line, offer up
your goodnight wishes

from the centre of the lawn.
I forget my calendar

of scars, so eager are you
for the next night and the next,

your palm reaching
for its milky light.

We turn to scale stairs,
come to the cot's edge

where I set you down
on the low tide of your day.

Taking You There

Parked up by the dunes, we tucked you
into your pram, pulled on our wellington boots.

We pushed towards the sea, lifted you
over the final rise, dropped down onto pebbles

and the deserted beach. For a time we just stood there,
facing the spray, before deciding the best way

was to free you from straps and carry you in.
Your father held you tight against his coat,

his spare hand locked in mine.
We waded forward, into the same cold pull

that took the ashes of your sister,
and lifted you above our heads.

Your baby's face was blustered by the wind
and we cried beneath your gasping laughs

as waves splashed inside our boots.
The unimaginable thought of you, last time

we were here, when we turned our backs and left her,
eddying in the tug. Ashore, I pushed the pram

but your father carried you back to the car,
unwilling to give up your squirming limbs.

Last Poem

So extraordinary was your sister's
short life, it's hard for me to see

a future for you. I know it's there,
your horizon of adulthood,

reachable across a stretch
of ordinary days, yet I can't believe

my fortune – to have a healthy child
with all that waits: the bike, school,

mild and curable diseases.
So we potter through the weeks

and you relax your simian cling,
take exploratory steps, language

budding at your lips. I log the daily
change, another day lived

with every kiss goodnight; wake
relieved by your murmurs at dawn.

Come and hold my hand, little one,
stand beside me in your small shoes,

let's head for your undiscovered life,
your mother's ready now, let's run.

Acknowledgements

Thanks are due to the editors of the following publications in which some of these poems – or versions of them – first appeared: *14 Magazine, Envoi, The Human Genre Project* (online), *Magma, Mslexia, The Reader, Shadowtrain* (online), *Stand.*

'A Child Dies in Liverpool' was selected for 'Perfect Places 2', North West libraries/Time to Read project 2012–2013.

'Echo' and 'Another' were broadcast on *Woman's Hour*, BBC Radio 4, May 2009.

'Her Birth', 'Toast', 'Print', 'I Sweat When I', 'Fetal Heart' and 'Another' were awarded third prize in the New Writer Prose and Poetry Prizes 2009 (collection category).

'In Memory of John Ernest Goss 1920–2011' was Highly Commended in the Crabbe Poetry Competition 2012.

'Lost' was shortlisted for both the Bridport Prize 2011 and the Mslexia Women's Poetry Competition 2012. It was a prizewinner in the Troubadour International Poetry Prize 2012.

'Muscovado Sugar' was longlisted for the Plough Prize 2011.

'Print' was Highly Commended in the Aesthetica Creative Arts Competition 2009.

'Ward at Night' was awarded second prize in Final Chapters: The Dying Matters Creative Writing Competition, 2012.

'Why We Had Another Baby' was published in *Not Only the Dark – 160 Poems on the Theme of Survival*, ed. Nicky Gould and Jo Field, WordAid.org.uk, 2011.